WOLFGANG AMADEUS MOZART

CONCERTO

for Piano and Orchestra
B♭ major/B-Dur/Si♭ majeur
K 595

Cadenzas by the Composer
Edited by/Herausgegeben von
Friedrich Blume

T0105992

Ernst Eulenburg Ltd

London · Mainz · Madrid · New York · Paris · Prague · Tokyo · Toronto · Zürich

I

W.A. MOZART

PIANO CONCERTO B ♭ MAJOR (KOECHEL No. 595)

The present opus, written down in the first days of 1791, forms the last link of a long chain. In the sphere of the piano concerto Mozart had developed his most prolific activity in the period preceding "The Marriage of Figaro" (1786). At that time the peculiarly romantic concerto in C minor (491) had given a certain finality to this work. In 1786 a straggler had followed in the C major concerto (503). Then various other interests came to the fore; trios, string quintets and vocal compositions displaced the piano concerto. The only one Mozart wrote after "Don Giovanni" was that in D major (537, the so-called "Coronation Concerto"). Subsequently the piano concerto recedes altogether for a period of three years. The last three symphonies, the last trios, the Trio-Divertimento, the string quartets for Friedrich Wilhelm II of Prussia, the clarinet quintet in A major and the string quintet in D major were the outcome. Only then, shortly after "Così fan tutte" (1790) and just before "The Magic Flute" (1791), Mozart made his last contribution —Koechel No. 595—to the category he had so richly cultivated and which for him had become a vehicle for decisive developments.

Jahn, and after him Koechel, only found praise for the "solemn, mild attitude" and the "magnificent harmony" in this concerto. Abert felt as being characteristic— compared with the earlier concertos— "the far more personal and at the same time strangely resigned tenor", that of "rousing himself and again relapsing"[1]). Probably the decisive impression, also for the present-day listener, is the serene clearness which the entire concerto radiates. The former tendency to set up marked contrasts and to enforce the unity of the whole by overcoming them, evidently gives way to the intention not to endanger this unity from the very outset.

The loosely scattered abundance of thematic ideas, already in the first orchestral *tutti*, hardly contains contrasts; everything grows like leaves, blossoms and fruits, plant-like as it were, from the stem. The only introductory bar (anticipating Schubert) already vouchsafes the steady flow of the movement and the whole composition. The romantic play with the dimness of the minor key (bar 50 seq.),

---

[1]) O. Jahn, Mozart, 4th edition (Deiters), 1907, II, p. 555; H. Abert, Mozart, 1921, II, p. 725 seq.

already favoured in the concerto 503, remains a characteristic also of this concerto. Thematic work and figuration in the piano part grow in a similarly organic manner, like rich vegetation. Here again the abundance of ideas hardly conveys any contrast (e. g. the episode in the minor key, bar 99 seq.), one might even say hardly anything novel. Mozarts previous richness of contrast, and the method of logic development of ideas from a central neucleus, adopted from Haydn, has been replaced, increasingly since the concertos 482 and 488, by a seemingly effortless and weightless play with matter. It reaches its ultimate maturity in Koechel No. 595.

As if unintentionally, and hardly noticeable, the constituent parts are interlinked: again and again motifs of the first *tutti* surround new thematic formations. The symphonic structure of the concerto, for which Mozart struggled so hard at one time, has disappeared. But also the "concerto manner" proper, whose life elements are rooted in the struggle of contrasts, has vanished. All is resolved into the unity of relaxed, unrestrained play. Even the orchestration allows no sense of contrast to creep in. Only infinitely fine shadings and gradations, most subtle transitions, produce the tonal mixture. Everything appears veiled by a slight haze which dims colours and tints. "In its colourful reflections we have life itself". Iridescent transparency, impalpable reflection, have displaced the former sanguine objectivity. It is hardly irony or resignation, but rather blissful sublimity, detached remoteness from earthly things

from which the master's weary body was to depart only a few months hence.

The simple *Lied* character of the themes is striking. It resolves the formerly favoured intricate structure of the theme into straightforward, classic lines leading directly up to "The Magic Flute" and the "Requiem". A creation such as the little wind episode, 1st movement bar 157 seq., (in the technique of composition merely a final group) radiates all the noble harmony of Sarastro's realm. It is characteristic that even the partly rather remote turns to the minor key in the "development" (bar 184 seq.) —as far as we can speak of one—and the linking of the piano figurations with the thematic fragments in bar 200 seq., at no time convey the same tenseness as does, for instance, the concerto 466, not even the glittering colour effects of 488. Everything takes its course in the perfect composure of natural, ideal beauty. A transition such as that in bars 228—235 of the 1st movement probably remains unrivalled in its serene tranquillity even by Mozart himself in somewhat earlier days.

The gaiety of the third movement dispels all doubts that again everything is set on evenness, flow and unity. Contrasts are hardly noticeable. Everything is embedded in the smiling relaxation of the $^6/_8$ theme which, alike the *tutti* motifs at the beginning of the 1st movement, surrounds the entire finale with unifying serenity. Again Schubert is not very far off.

In such environments the middle movement can impossibly aim at a contrast. It again is dominated by placid composure and blissful sublimity. The prescribed notation $\math$ (all older editions wrongly show $\mathbf{C}$) explicitly secures flowing movement for the "Larghetto". In this "peaceful" concerto the middle movement is the place of the holiest tranquillity. The noble grandeur must be endangered neither by dynamic exaggerations nor by too broad tempi. All emotions, everything humanly unessential, has dropped off. There is neither grief nor joy, neither irony nor despair, neither resignation nor consolation. In the world of this "noble simplicity and peaceful grandeur" emotions are vain.

With such an opus Mozart's piano concerto work takes an end, rising smilingly above the feigned world of reality, above truth and error. What the dramatist Mozart achieved in "Così fan tutte" with the ironic rendering of reality, and in „The Magic Flute" with the realisation of an ideal world, that he achieves as instrumental composer with the means of this concerto: the conquest of life.

The revision was based on the autograph (Prussian State Library, Berlin) and the Complete Edition (Breitkopf & Härtel). As in the case of the earlier concertos the Complete Edition again proves to be a revised reprint of the older printed editions. The first edition of the concerto in B♭ major, Koechel 595, was published by Artaria in Vienna already in 1791 (platenumber 346, advertised in the „Wiener Zeitung" of August 13th). A reprint of the Artaria edition was issued in 1792 by Hummel in Amsterdam as Op. V, lib. 1, plate-

number 763. André in Offenbach only followed as the third publisher in 1800 and included the concerto in his collection "Six grands concertos dédiés au Prince Louis Ferdinand de Prusse" as No. 2 and as opus 82, plate-number 1416. His edition partly reverts again to the original[1]).

Mozart's cadenzas for the 1st and 3rd movements (Koechel Nos. 624, 34—36), as printed in the Complete Edition of Mozart's works, are taken from the older editions by Artaria and André[2]). As neither the autographs nor any other sources are known, they were included in the present edition unchanged.

As all the others of Mozart's piano concertos, the present one also requires thorough bass accompaniment throughout. The autograph demands it page for page. The left hand in the piano part regularly follows the string bass and only pauses when that is silent. Passages such as bars 158—162 in the 1st movement are to be rendered without thorough bass because the string basses are silent. Occasionally, however, the thorough bass accompaniment pauses in places where the string basses continue to play, e. g. 2nd movement, bars 127—129. That passages such as bars 105—106 in the 1st movement, or bar 49 seq. of the second movement, require chordic supplementation in the left hand follows as a matter of course. In the concerto 595 the differentiation between tutti and soli in the string orchestra is carefully noted. All solo passages of the piano should be accom-

---

[1]) For the printed editions cp. Deutsch and Oldman, Zeitschrift f. Musikwiss. XIV, pp. 150, 338, 341 and 348.

[2]) Koechel No. 624, under „Ausgaben".

panied only by the *soli* of the strings. Even such short accompaniments as bars 154—156 and 166—167 in the 1st movement require this treatment. Occasionally wind solos are also accompanied by the string *soli* alone, thus in bars 198—199 of the 1st movement where Mozart noted „solo" in all string parts, but then crossed it out again for the bass, letting it stand only for 1st and 2nd violins and viola. Certain notations only become plausible by way of this practice of changing between *tutti* and *soli*, e. g. 1st movement, bars 140—145: in this instance the rests marked under the notes of the bass part do not indicate *"violoncelli"*, but *"soli"*. That all directions in the autograph are given with minutest care, almost with pedantic exactness, is a matter of course with Mozart.

Prof. Dr. Friedrich Blüme.

W.A. MOZART

KLAVIERKONZERT B-DUR K.-V. No. 595)

Das vorliegende Werk, in den ersten Tagen des Jahres 1791 niedergeschrieben, bildet das Endglied einer langen Reihe. Auf dem Gebiete des Klavierkonzerts hatte Mozart seine fruchtbarste Tätigkeit in der Zeit vor „Figaros Hochzeit" (1786) entfaltet. Mit dem seltsam romantischen Konzert in c-moll (491) hatte damals diese Arbeit einen gewissen Abschluß gefunden. Noch 1786 war ihr in dem Konzert in C-dur (503) ein Nachzügler entstanden. Dann schoben mancherlei andere Interessen sich in den Vordergrund. Klaviertrios, Streichquintette, Gesangswerke verdrängten das Klavierkonzert. Nach dem „Don Giovanni" schrieb Mozart als einziges Klavierkonzert dasjenige in D-dur (537, sog. „Krönungskonzert"). In der folgenden Zeit trat für drei Jahre das Klavierkonzert ganz zurück. Die letzen drei Symphonien, die letzten Klaviertrios, das Trio-Divertimento, die Streichquartette für Friedrich Wilhelm II. von Preußen, das Klarinettenquintett in A-dur und das Streichquintett in D-dur entstanden. Erst dann, kurz nach „Così fan tutte" (1790) und kurz vor der „Zauberflöte" (1791) lieferte Mozart mit K.-V. 595 den letzten

Beitrag zu der von ihm so besonders reich gepflegten Gattung, die für ihn zum Gefäß so entscheidender Wandlung geworden war.

Jahn und nach ihm Köchel wußten an dem Konzert nur die „ernst milde Haltung" und den „herrlichen Wohlklang" zu rühmen. Abert empfand den — im Vergleich zu den früheren Konzerten — „weit persönlicheren und dabei merkwürdig resignierten Ton", das „Sichaufraffen und Zurücksinken" als charakteristisch[1]. Vielleicht ist doch der entscheidende Eindruck, auch für den heutigen Hörer, die ruhige Klarheit, die das ganze Konzert ausströmt. Die frühere Neigung, stark zugespitzte Gegensätze aufzutürmen und die Einheit des Ganzen durch deren Überwindung zu erzwingen, weicht hier offensichtlich dem Bestreben, die Einheit von vornherein gar nicht in Frage zu stellen.

Die locker hingestreute Fülle der thematischen Einfälle, gleich im ersten Orchestertutti, enthält kaum Kontraste: alles wächst wie Blatt, Blüte und Frucht, gleichsam pflanzenhaft aus dem Stamm. Der einzige Einleitungstakt (Schubert vor-

---

[1] O. Jahn, Mozart, 4. Aufl. (Deiters), 1907, II, S. 555; H. Abert, Mozart, 1921, II, S. 725 f.

wegnehmend) gibt schon die Gewähr für das ruhige Strömen des ganzen Satzes und Werkes. Das romantische Spiel mit der Molltrübung (T. 50 ff.), das schon das Konzert 503 liebte, bleibt ein Kennzeichen auch für dieses Konzert. Die Klavierthematik und -figuration wächst ähnlich organisch wie üppige Vegetation. Auch hier wird die Menge der Einfälle nicht gegensätzlich empfunden (so etwa der Moll-Seitensatz, T. 99 ff.), ja vielleicht kaum als neuartig wahrgenommen. An die Stelle von Mozarts früherem Kontrastreichtum und an die Stelle des Haydn nachgebildeten Verfahrens einer logischen Gedankenentwicklung aus dem zentralen Ansatz heraus hat sich, zunehmend etwa seit den Konzerten 482 und 488, das scheinbar mühelose und gewichtlose Spiel mit der Materie geschoben. Es erlebt in K.-V. 595 seine letzte Reife.

Wie unabsichtlich und kaum spürbar schieben sich die Glieder ineinander: Motive des ersten Tutti umschließen immer wieder die thematischen Neubildungen. Verschwunden ist die symphonische Anlage des Konzerts, um die Mozart eine Zeitlang so heiß gerungen hatte. Verschwunden ist aber auch das eigentliche „Konzertwesen", das ja im Kampf der Gegensätze sein Lebenselement besitzt. Hier geht alles in der Einheit eines gelösten, freien Spieles auf. Auch die Instrumentierung läßt kein Gefühl eines Gegensatzes aufkommen. Nur unendlich feine Schattierungen und Stufungen, zarteste Übergänge bringen die Klangmischungen hervor. Alles erscheint wie in den Schleier eines leichten Dunstes getaucht, der alle Farben mildert, alle

Töne dämpft. „Am farbigen Abglanz haben wir das Leben". Schillernde Transparenz, untastbare Spiegelung haben die frühere blutvolle Gegenständlichkeit verdrängt. Kaum ist es Ironie, kaum Resignation zu nennen, eher eine selige Erhabenheit, eine abgelöste Ferne vom Irdischen, dem des Meisters müder Leib ja auch schon wenige Monate später entrückt werden sollte.

Auffallend ist die schlichte Liedhaftigkeit der Themen. Sie löst die frühere in sich verwickelte Struktur des Themas in geradlinige Klassizität und gemahnt unmittelbar an „Zauberflöte" und „Requiem". Ein Gebilde wie die kleine Bläserepisode, 1. Satz, T. 157 ff. (kompositionstechnisch nichts als eine Schlußgruppe) strömt ganz die edle Harmonie von Sarastros Reich aus. Bezeichnend, daß selbst die zum Teil recht abgelegenen Mollwendungen der „Durchführung" — soweit man von einer solchen sprechen kann — T. 184 ff. und die Verknüpfung der Klavierfiguration mit den Themenbruchstücken T. 200 ff. nirgends den gespannten Eindruck etwa des Konzerts 466 verursachen, ja nicht einmal die schillernden Farbwirkungen von 488 hervorbringen. Alles vollzieht sich in der vollendeten Gelassenheit einer natürlich-idealischen Schönheit. Ein Übergang wie 1. Satz T. 228—235 dürfte selbst bei Mozart wenig früher an abgeklärter Ruhe seinesgleichen suchen.

Die heitere Laune des dritten Satzes kann doch keine Täuschung darüber aufkommen lassen, daß auch hier alles auf Gleichmaß, Fluß, Einheit abgestimmt ist. Gegensätze werden auch hier kaum spürbar. Alles ist in die lächelnde Gelöstheit des $^6/_8$-Themas eingebettet, das, wie im 1. Satz die Tuttimotive des Anfangs, das ganze Finale mit einigender Ruhe umschließt. Auch hier steht Schubert nicht fern.

In solcher Umgebung kann auch der Mittelsatz nicht als Kontrast angelegt sein. Ruhige Gelassenheit und selige Erhabenheit beherrschen auch ihn. Das „Larghetto" wird durch die Vorschrift des ₵ (alle älteren Ausgaben haben fälschlich C) ausdrücklich zu sehr fließender Bewegung gebracht. In diesem „stillen" Konzert ist der Mittelsatz der Ort heiligster Stille. Die noble Überlegenheit darf weder durch dynamische Übertreibungen noch durch eine zu breite Temponahme gefährdet werden. Alle Erregung, alles Menschlich-Unwesentliche ist hier abgefallen. Es gibt weder Trauer noch Freude, weder Ironie noch Verzweiflung, weder Resignation noch Trost. In der Welt dieser „edlen Einfalt und stillen Größe" sind Affekte wesenlos.

Mit einem solchen Werk schließt das Klavierkonzertschaffen Mozarts ab, in letzter lächelnder Erhebung über die Scheinwelt des Wirklichen, über Wahrheit und Irrtum. Was der Dramatiker Mozart in „Così fan tutte" durch die Ironisierung der Realität, in der „Zauberflöte" durch die Verwirklichung einer idealen Welt, das gestaltet der Instrumentalkomponist Mozart mit den Mitteln dieses Konzerts: die Überwindung des Lebens.

Die Revision erfolgte auf Grund des Autographs (Preußische Staatsbibliothek, Berlin) und der Gesamtausgabe (Breitkopf & Härtel). Die Gesamtausgabe erweist sich auch im Falle des vorliegenden Konzerts, wie bei den früheren, als ein überarbeiteter Nachdruck der älteren Druckausgaben. Die Erstausgabe des Konzerts B-dur 595 brachte Artaria in Wien unter der Verlags-Nummer 346 schon im Jahre 1791 heraus (angezeigt in der „Wiener Zeitung" am 13. August). 1792 erfolgte ein Nachdruck nach Artaria durch Hummel in Amsterdam unter der Bezeichnung op. V, lib. 1, und der Verlags-Nummer 763. Erst als dritter Verleger folgte André in Offenbach im Jahre 1800, der das Konzert in seiner Sammlung „Six grands Concertos dédiés au Prince Louis Ferdinand de Prusse" als Nr. 2 unter der Opuszahl 82 und der Verlags-Nummer 1416 druckte; seine Ausgabe geht zum Teil wieder auf das Original zurück [1]).

Mozarts Kadenzen zum 1. und 3. Satz (K.-V. 624, Nr. 34—36) sind in der Gesamtausgabe der Werke Mozarts wiedergegeben nach den älteren Druckausgaben von Artaria und von André [2]). Da weder die Autographen noch weitere Quellen dazu bekannt sind, wurden sie von dort unverändert in die vorliegende Ausgabe übernommen.

Wie alle anderen Klavierkonzerte Mozarts rechnet auch das vorliegende mit durchgängiger Generalbaßbegleitung. Das Autograph fordert sie Seite für Seite. Die linke Hand des Klaviers geht ständig mit den Streichbässen und pausiert nur, wo diese schweigen. Stellen, wie z. B.

---

[1]) Zu den Druckausgaben vgl. Deutsch und Oldman, Zeitschr. f. Musikwiss. XIV, S. 150, 338, 341 und 348.

[2]) Köchel Nr. 624, unter „Ausgaben".

1. Satz, T. 158—162, sind, weil die Streichbässe pausieren, ohne Generalbaßbegleitung zu denken. Vereinzelt pausiert die Generalbaßbegleitung jedoch auch an Stellen, an denen die Streichbässe tätig sind, so z. B. 2. Satz, T. 127—129. Daß Stellen wie 1. Satz, T. 105—106, oder 2. Satz, T. 49 ff., in der linken Hand akkordisch zu füllen sind, versteht sich danach von selbst. Das Konzert 595 schreibt sehr genau im Streichorchester den Unterschied von Tutti und Solo vor. Alle Klaviersoli sollen von den Streichern nur solistisch begleitet werden. Selbst kurze Begleitstellen, wie 1. Satz, T. 154—156 und 166—167, sind so zu verstehen. Mitunter werden auch Bläsersoli nur von Solostreichern begleitet, so 1. Satz, T. 198-199, wo Mozart in allen Streichern „Solo" vorgeschrieben, dann aber für die Bässe diese Vorschrift durchstrichen und sie nur für Viol. I, II und Viola hat stehen lassen. Manche Notierungen werden nur aus dieser Praxis des Wechsels zwischen Tutti und Soli verständlich, so 1. Satz, T. 140—145: hier bedeutet in der Baßstimme die Pausensetzung unter den Noten nicht etwa „Violoncelli", sondern „Soli". Daß im übrigen die Anweisungen des Autographs von minutiöser Sorgfalt, ja fast pedantischer Exaktheit sind, ist für Mozart selbstverständlich.

Prof. Dr. Friedrich Blume.

E. E. 4899

Piano Concerto

I.

Allegro

W. A. Mozart
1756-1791
Köchel No. 595

E. E. 4899

2

4

5

6

* The next 7 bars which Mozart had forgotten in his MS. he added later on at the end, see p. 85

* Die nächsten 7 Takte, die Mozart im MS. vergessen, aber später am Schluss hinzugefügt hat, s. p. 85

8

10

E. E. 4899

E. E. 4899

12

E. E. 4899

14

22

E.E. 4899

28

30

32

E. E. 4899

34

E.E.4899

E.H.4899

II.

Larghetto

44

E.E.4899

46

50

* Mozart has cancelled the next 7 notes and noted Basso

* Mozart hat die folgenden 7 Noten gestrichen und notiert: Basso

III.

58

E.E. 4899

60

61

E.E. 4899

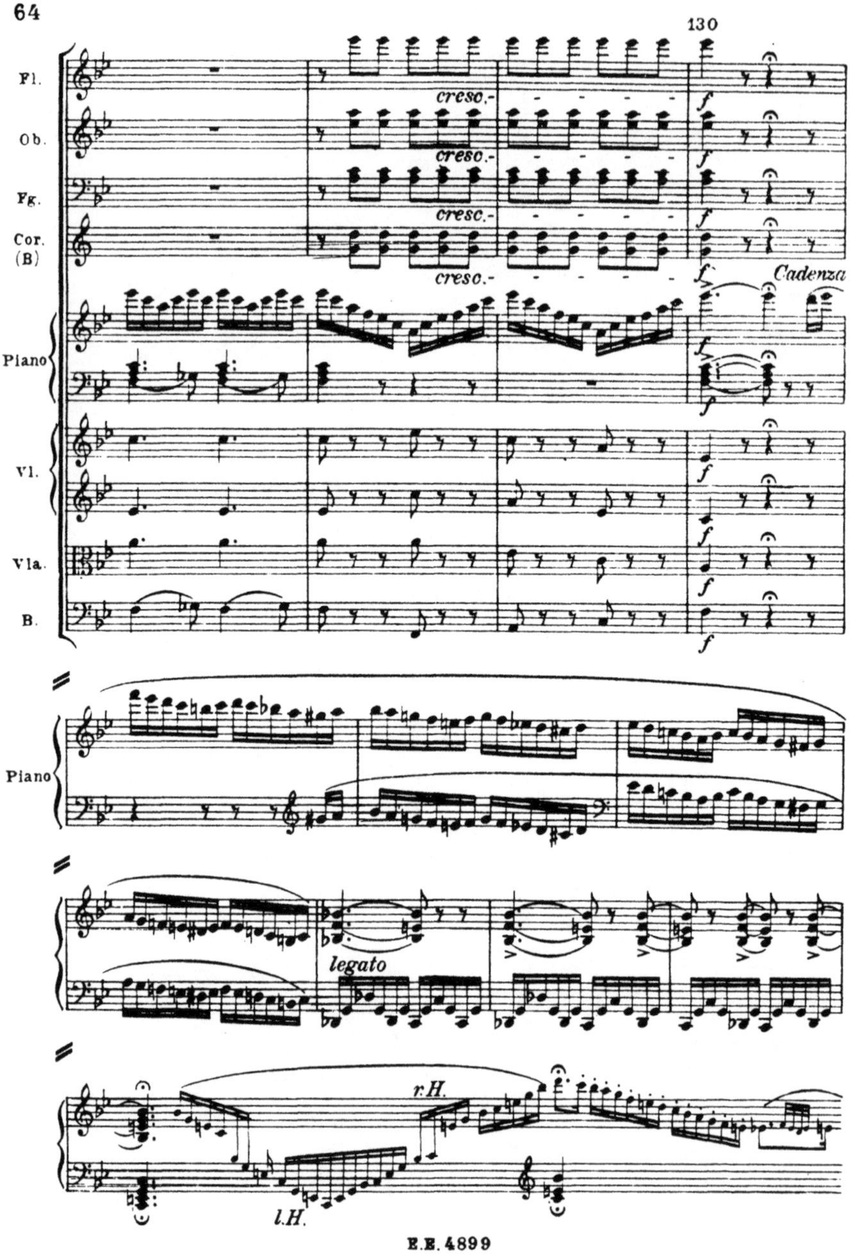
130
Fl.
Ob.
Fg.
Cor. (B)
Piano
Vl.
Vla.
B.
cresc.-
f
Cadenza
legato
r.H.
l.H.

66

E.E. 4899

74

E. E. 4899

84

E. E. 4899

To be inserted on p. 6 following bar 46

E.E. 4899